THIS BOOK BELONGS TO:

Test Your Colors Here

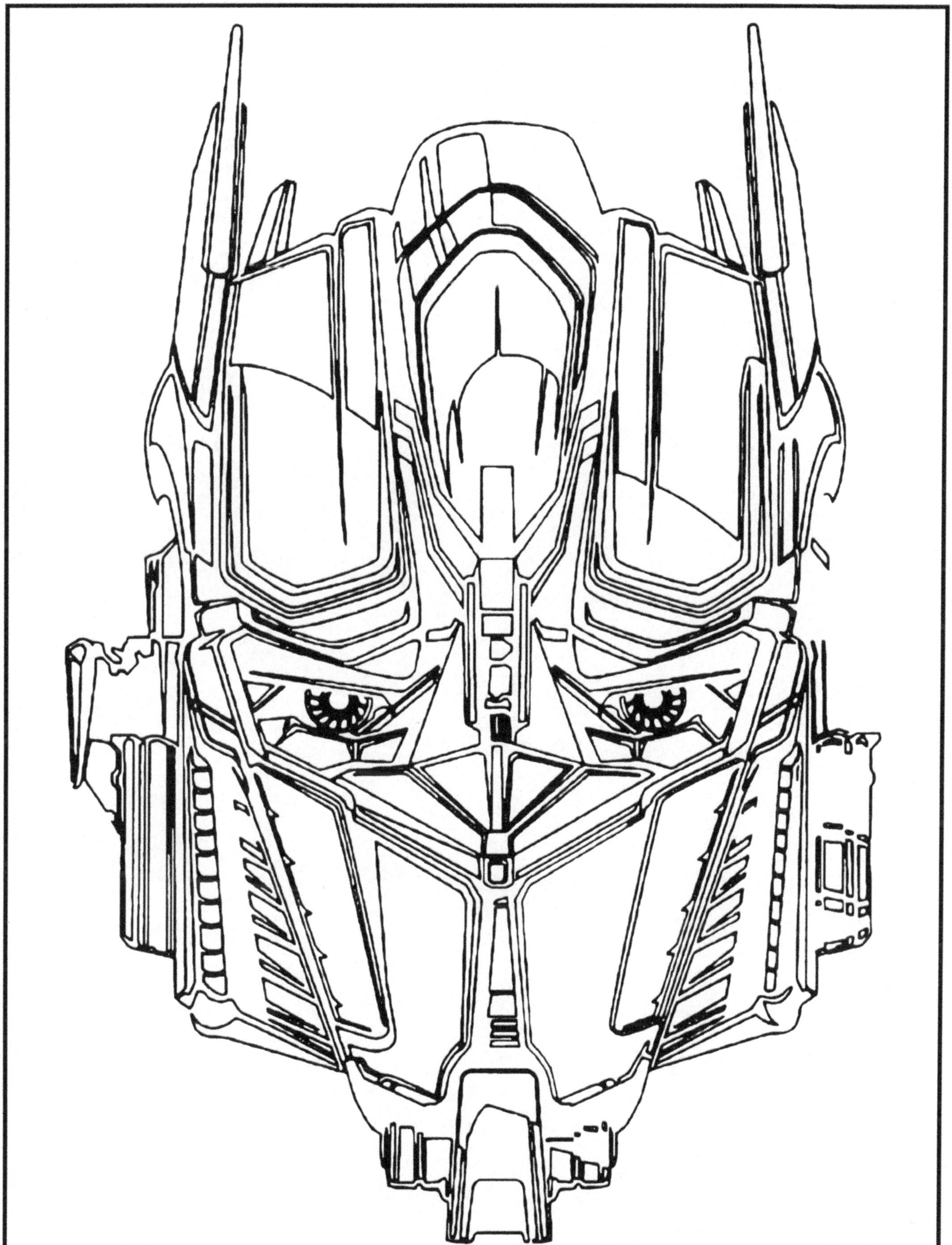

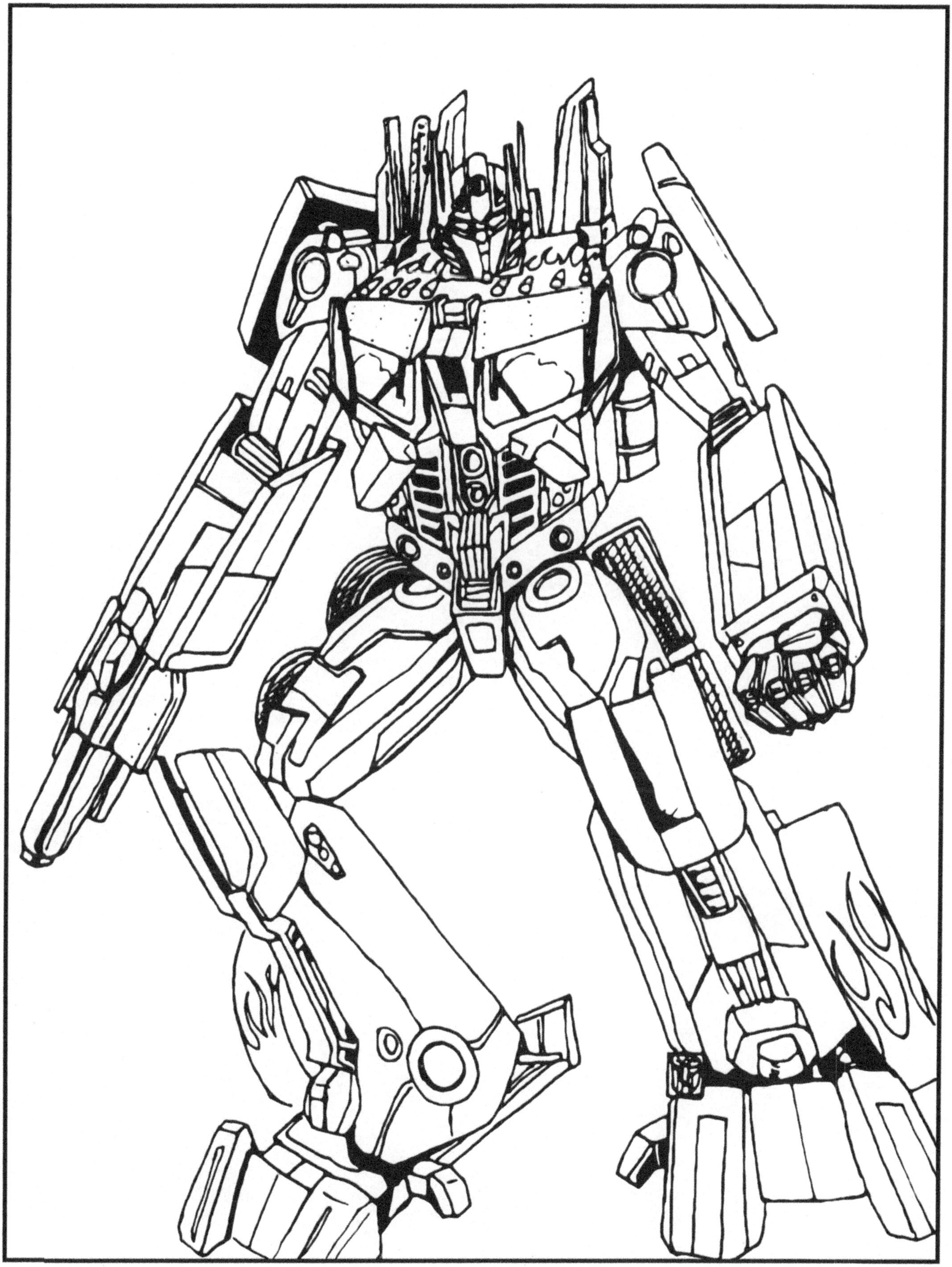

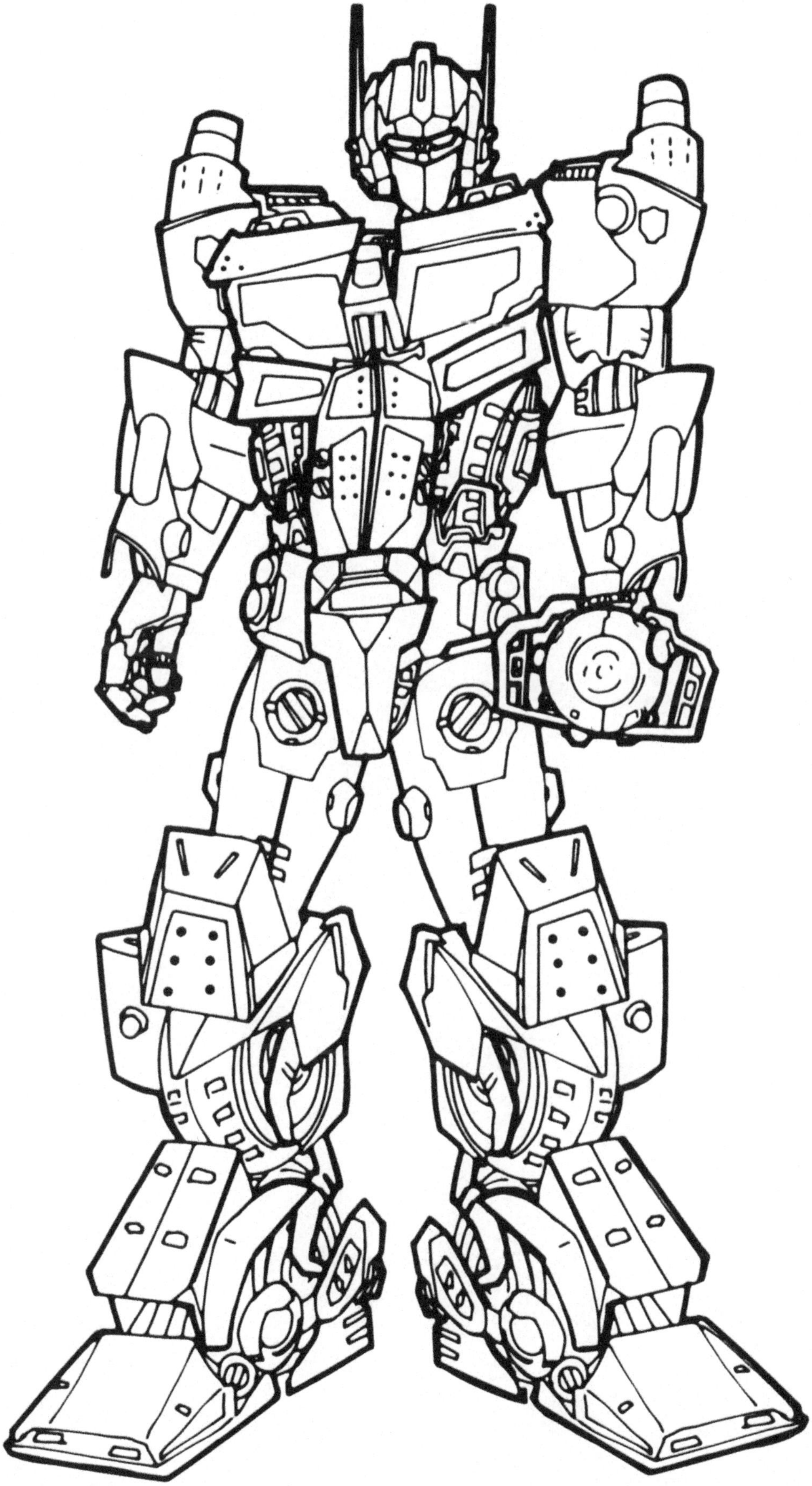

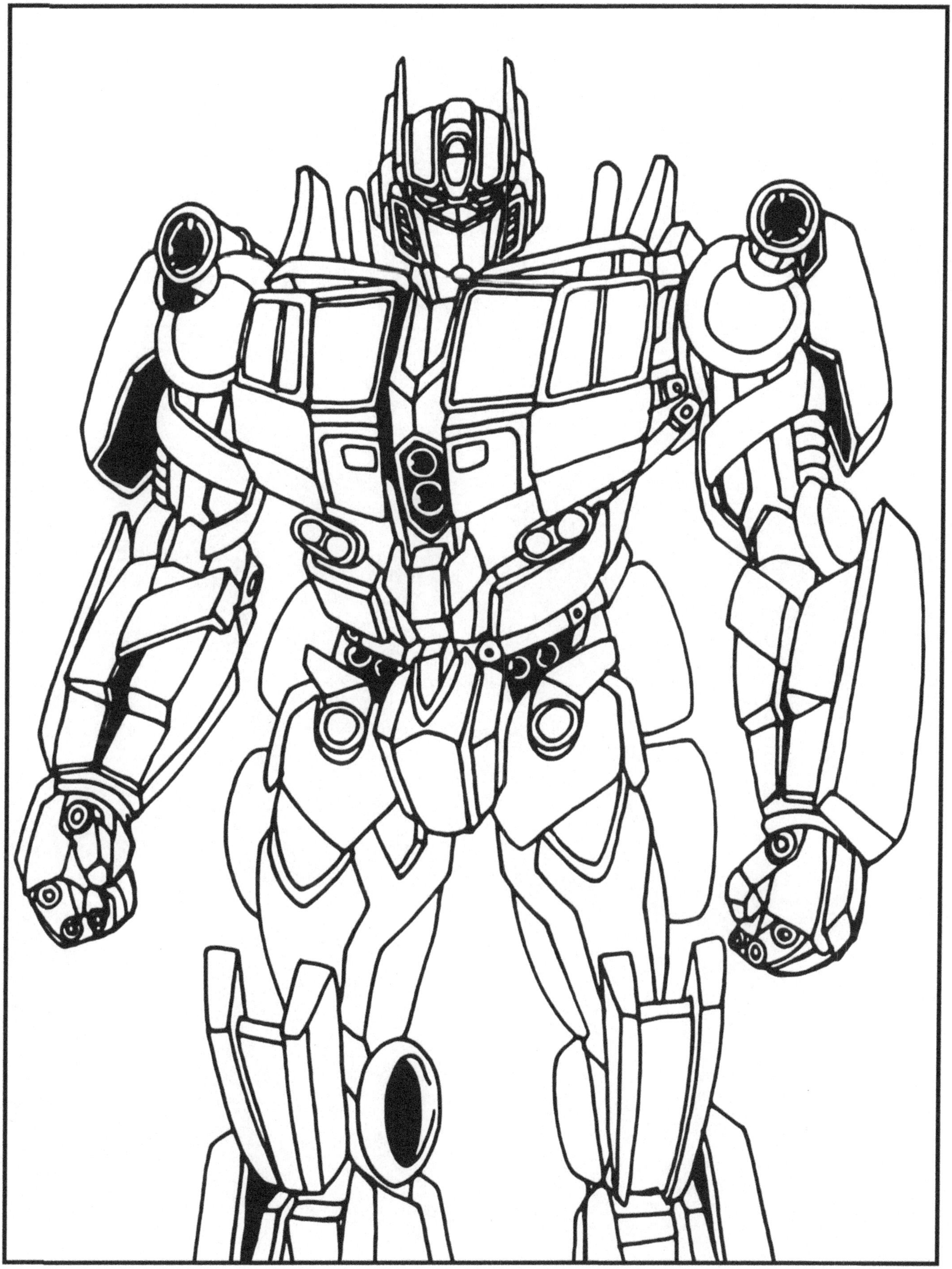

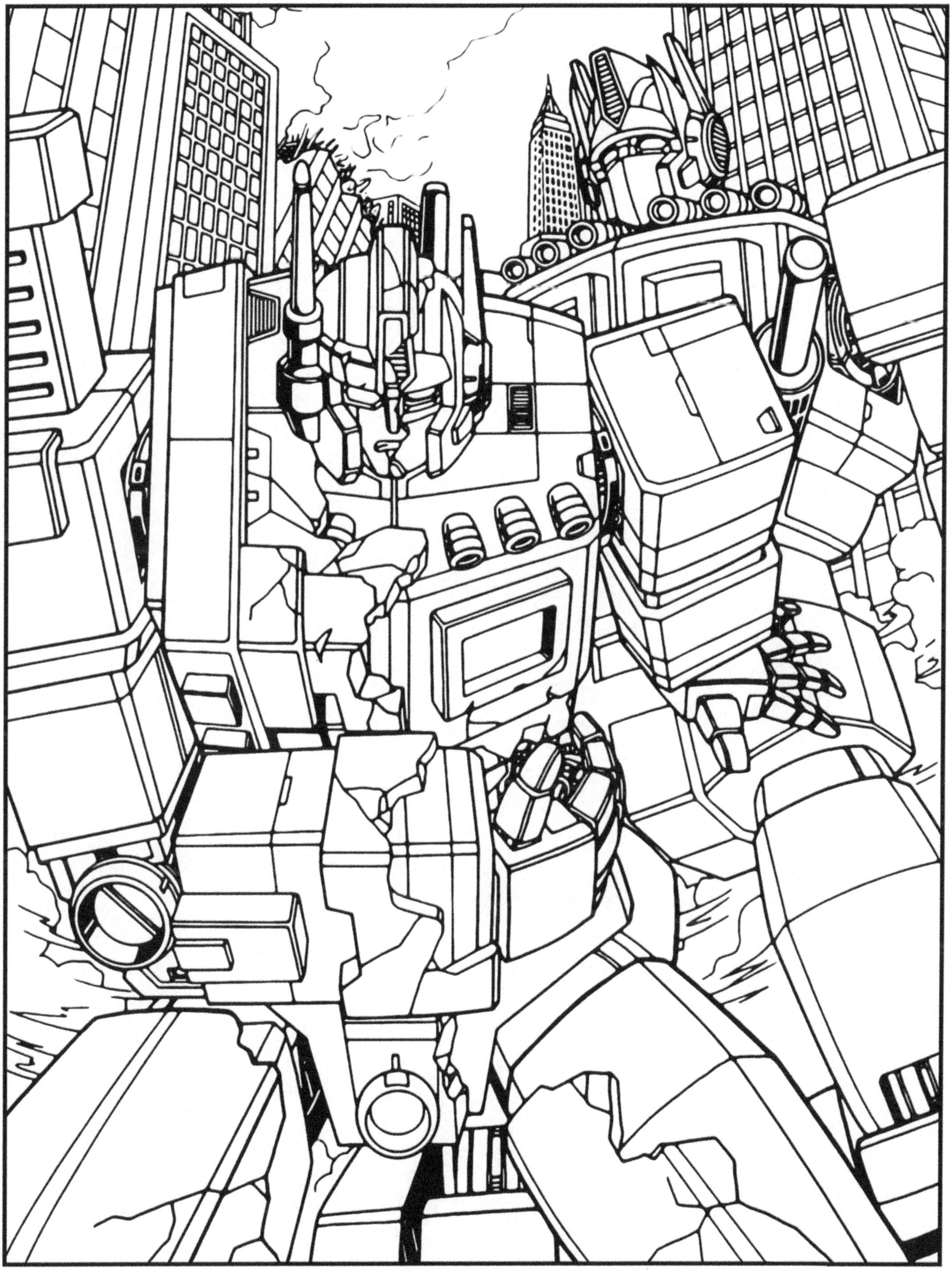

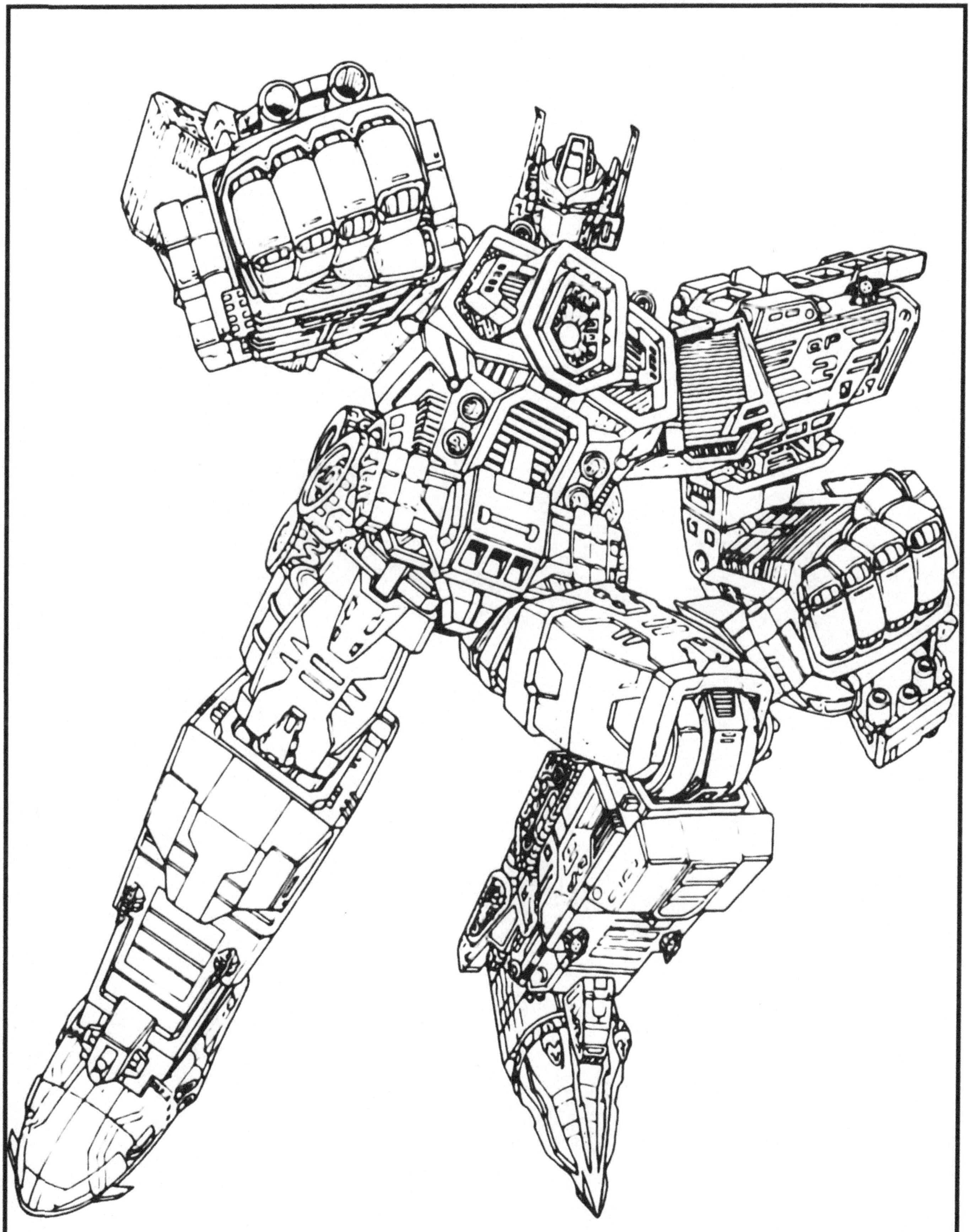

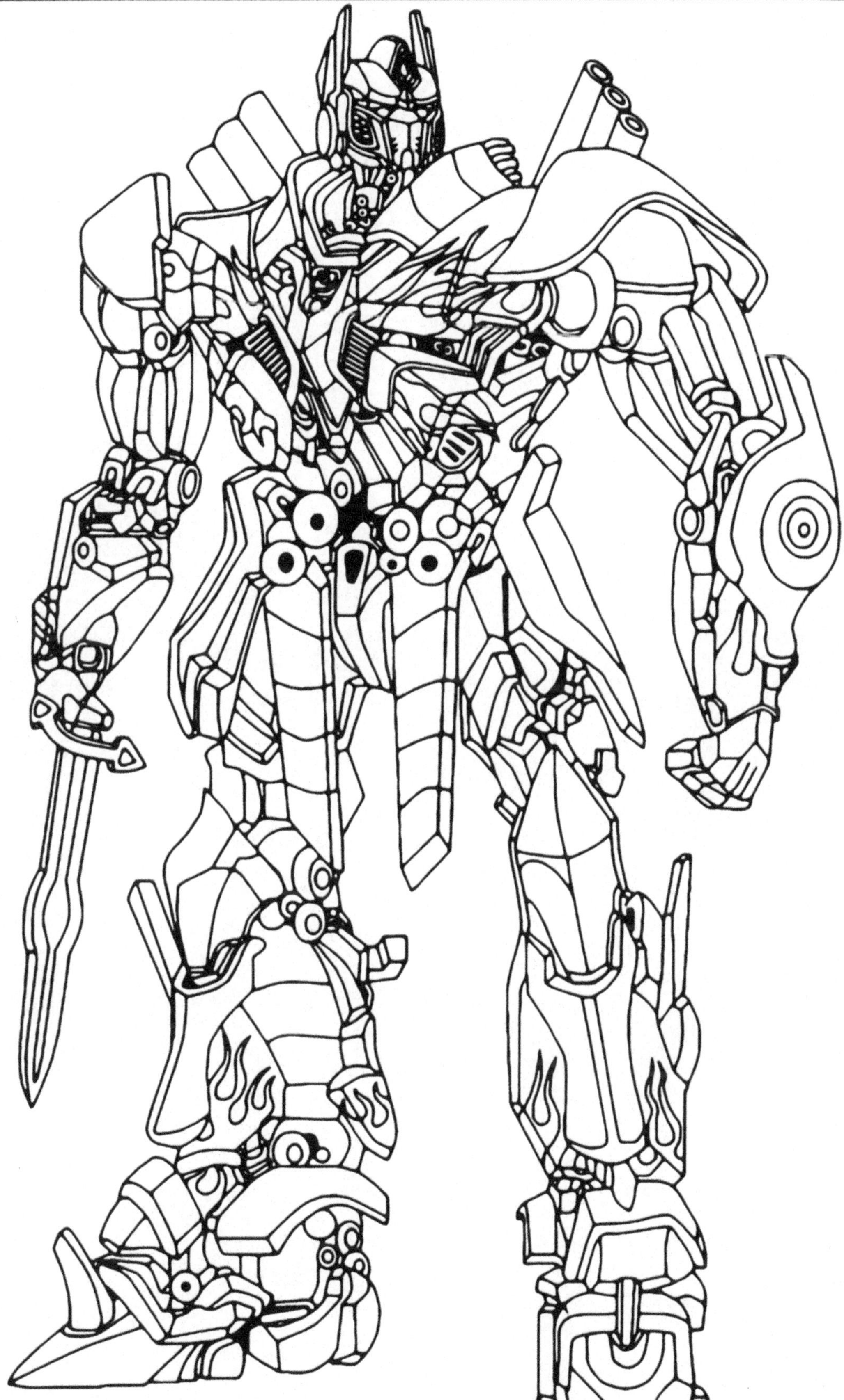

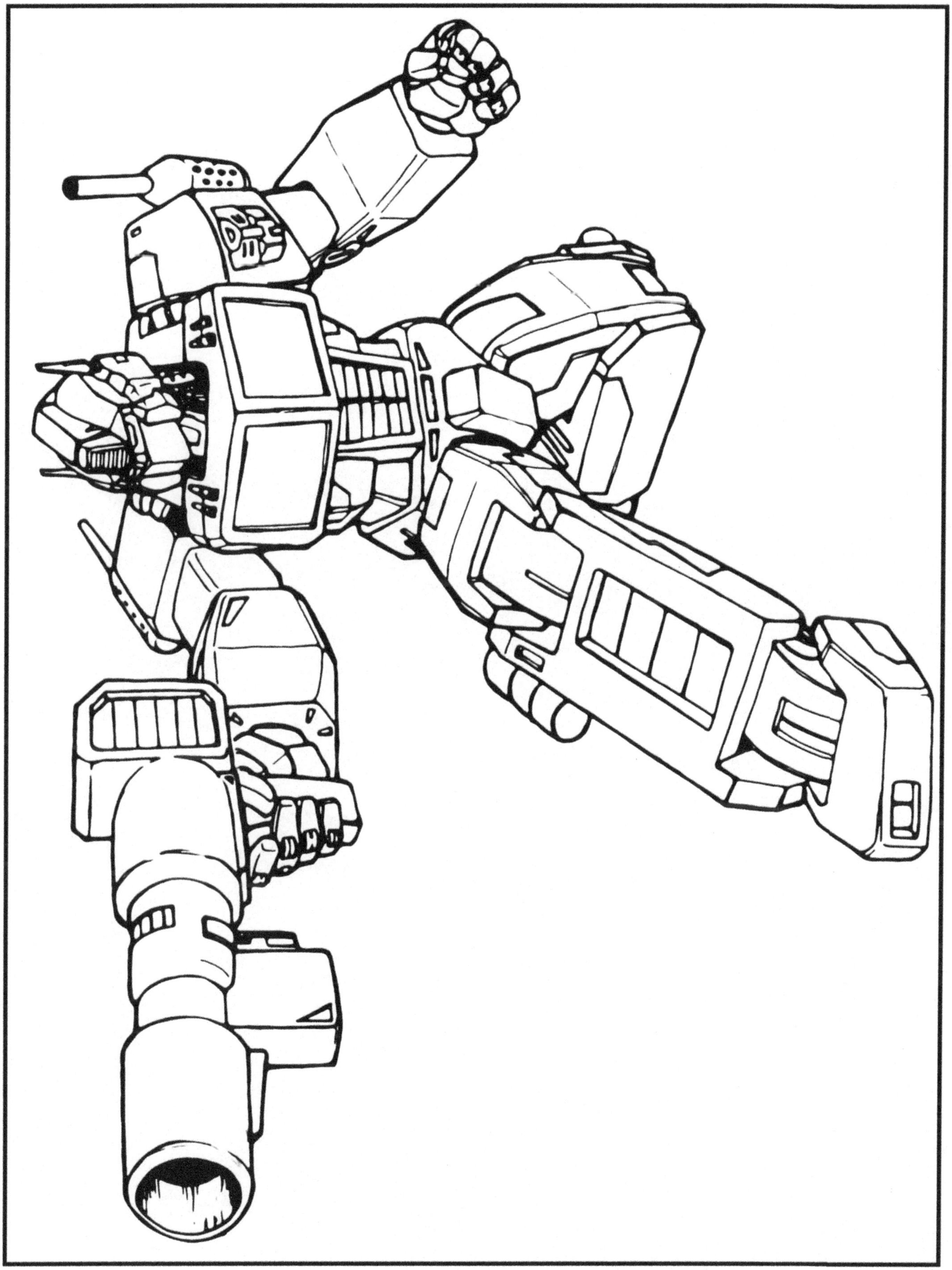

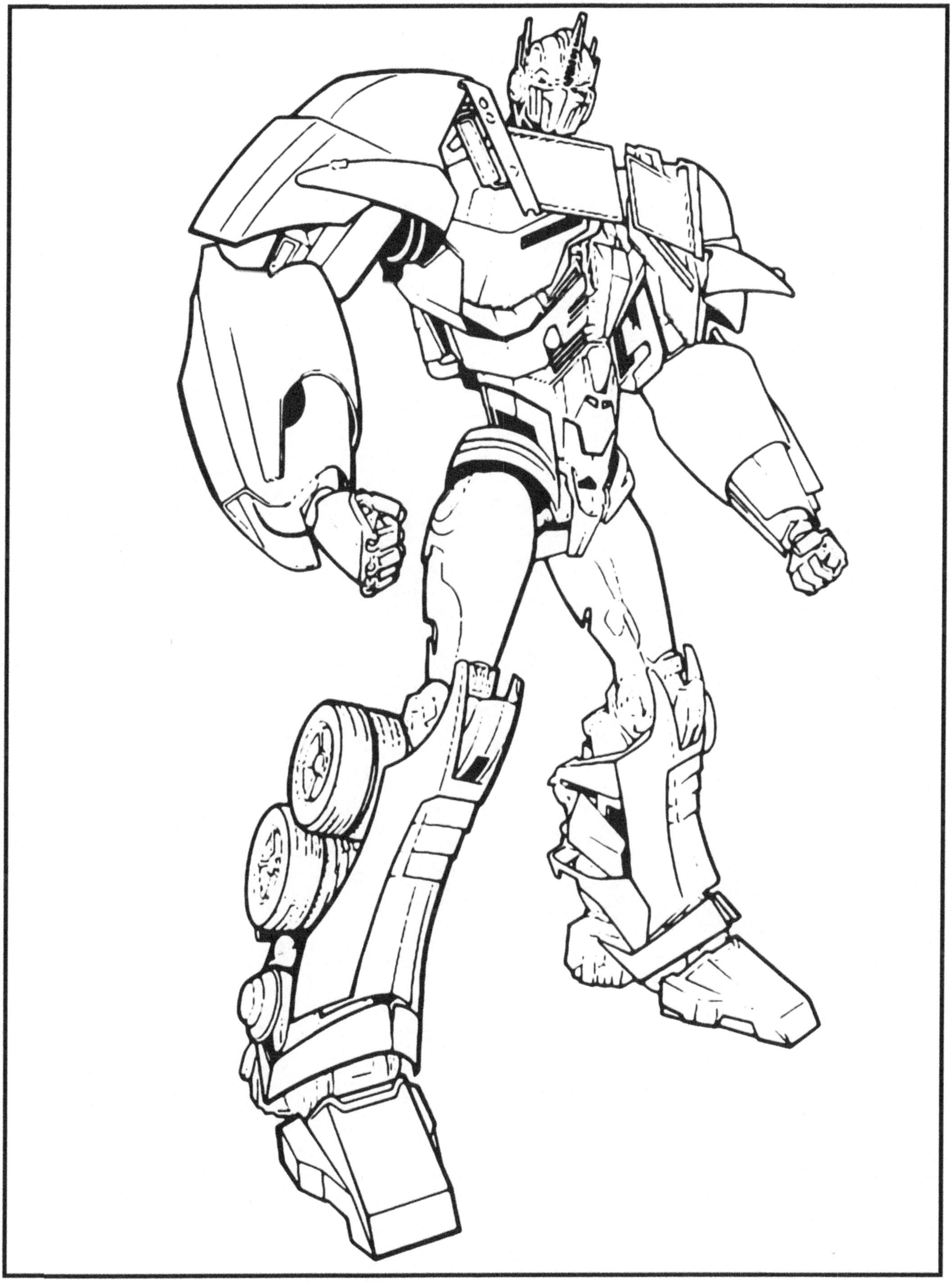

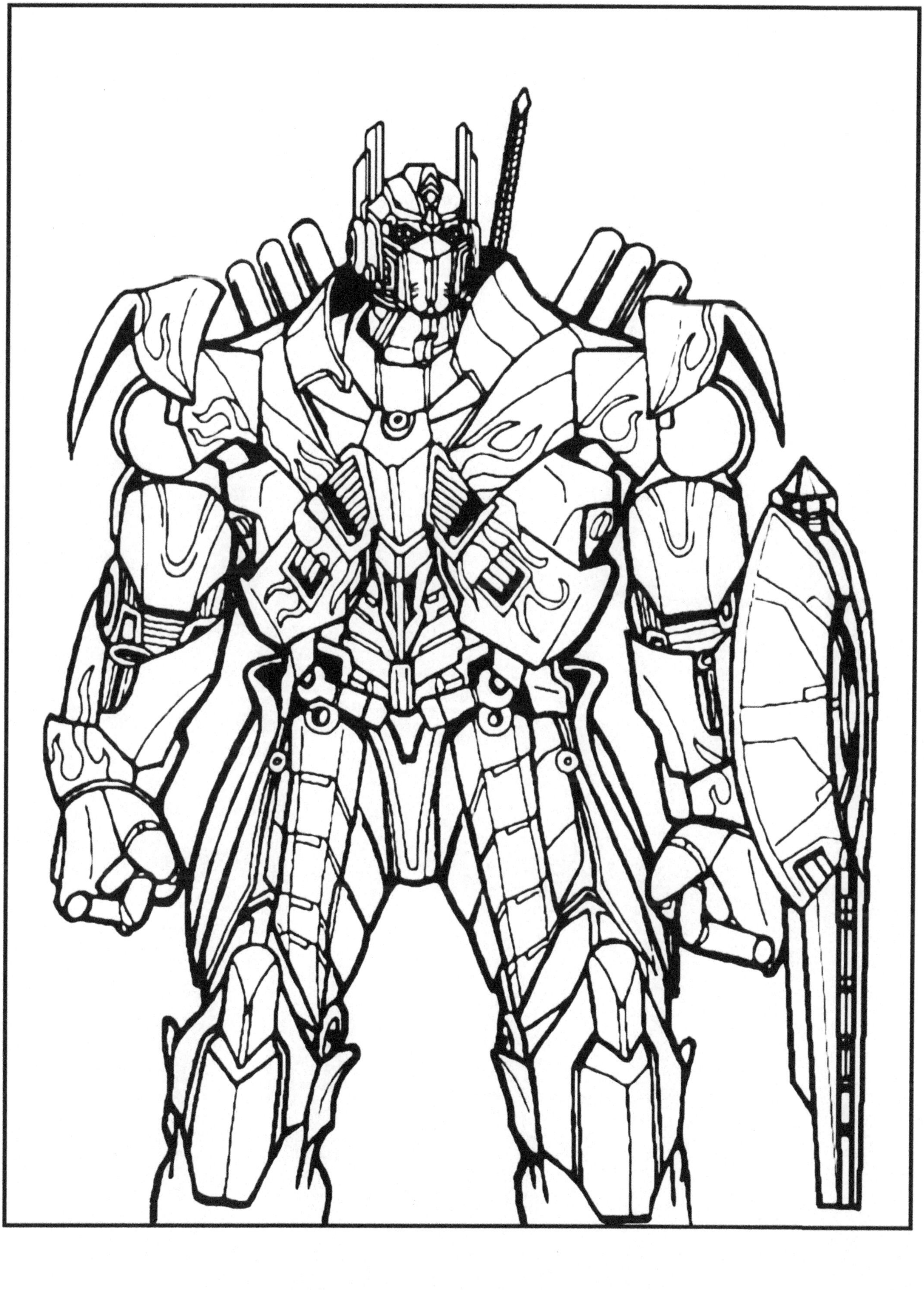